Other books by
Stewart S. Warren

———————————

Shape of a Hill

The Weight of Dusk

Second Light

The Song of It:
A Travelogue of Norteño

Essence:
contemplations in image and word
with Corinna Stoeffl

The Sea Always Near

Just One Leaf

Atogaki

www.heartlink.com

Follow Hawk

Mercury HeartLink

Follow Hawk

poems for thriving

Stewart S. Warren

Follow Hawk: poems for thriving
Copyright ©2011 Stewart S. Warren

ISBN: 9780982730379
Publisher: Mercury HeartLink

Book design by Mercury HeartLink
Back cover portrait photograph by Georgia Santa-Maria
Front cover image: "Desert Passage" ©Kenneth Rougeau

Kenneth Rougeau is a digital artist, poet and musician who currently resides in Portland,
Oregon. He has created numerous surrealistic fantasy images and has also created collages
to illustrate both *Alice In Wonderland* and *Through The Looking Glass*.
See more of his work at: http://krougeau.artfire.com

These poems were written in the first half of 2011.

Mercury HeartLink
editor@heartlink.com

Additional copies and other HeartLink publications at: www.heartlink.com

Contents

Even with the Sun Turned On

Acorns for the Deer

Traffic Always Traffic

THE BLUE CURL WITHIN YOU

Recognize that you are
this love that you love.
Simple and endless. And here.

—Gangaji

UNASSUMING GUEST

Gladly Onward

This is where we'll be—in some kitchen
helping each other grow;
on the forward deck watching a shore
of galactic collision come into view;
trading bodies; making blue atmosphere.
This is where.

We'll rotate the libraries of time to ponder
the days before the Great Cooperation.
How we crawled and crawled,
passing the silver seed forward.
A tingle at the base of the spine
will remind us of fight, flight, bicuspids.
This is how.

The heart will be a poem, understood
but not conquered. A symbol of Earth
touched with reverence will
send courage into every now.
Peach trees and dragonflies accompany us.

Where we'll be... calls us forward.
Where we are... is already forgiven.   ∽

SHRINE

When you visit a sacred shrine,
and are honest with yourself,
you know if the spirit remains
or has moved on. You know.

How many god's eyes are hung
in the trees, crosses tied with twigs and vine,
photos of soldiers and plastic roses?
How many kisses on the bell?

Take a half a handful of dirt,
a pebble, a card from the vendor,
any card, place it back in the deck—
is this the wish you came with?

A miracle is a bird
with better things on its mind.
A miracle walks at dawn
among the living and the dead.

A miracle might be pulled from this assignment
without replacement.
I'm praying at the feet of my own hope.
I'm standing in heartache's river.

There's lightning in the hills,
a frenzy of insects, songs
of the forsaken, smoke, nothing.
In another valley a surge of hot water

works its way to the surface,
innocent, discrete. A passerby
lays down his crooked body,
hears the holy binding music. ⤚

Unassuming Guest

Gentleness, once taunted and dismissed,
has found a way into our house.
It has survived. What had passed for it
was being nice and getting along.
    And let's face it, niceness is nice,
and getting along means you can leave
your bicycle outside the door,
hold a different opinion and not get slapped.

But gentleness, gentleness came the distance.
It traveled with train robbers, was the hostage
of bullies more times than we can count, was buried
repeatedly on the back pages of the Times.
    Second rate. Silenced.
We understand that now.

It's not holding our tongues, it's having tongues
that know the power of words.
It's when *yes* means *yes*, and *no* has no hidden knife.
Being with you, eventually, brought me
    to myself, to the proving ground.
You were there—my fists on the table,
my extra heavy steps. Nightmares.
I kept slamming my parents' doors;
I was a dog on my own chain.

But it wasn't all about me—we took turns.
Gentleness was the last door on the left.

Gentleness is a Navajo handshake.
It's a glass of water set down without advise.
It's just a few words, or none at all.
It's the eyes and hands and future relaxed.
Gentleness was there all along, gathering
in that sharp, dark, cluttered house. ᥦ

THE WISDOM OF KINGS
for Rick Smith

Winged and wounded on the bardic wheel
you cross into our small sky—
a hand to your heart
when you speak, timidity mixed
with outbound flights,
a yellow knife for camping.
You chose wrens.

That's how the story goes—
those little kings that rode
the shelves of parting land,
that nest in laundry hanging on the line,
that pick their meals from Arizona plates,
arrive, disarrive, leave
no trace in the sky.

I imagine their wisdom as a wave
that knows when to curl.
Their seed-sized hearts move
with the tides of our becoming.
Also... companions.
You are their spokesperson
and God knows every tribe needs a poet,
every poet a migration.

At three in the afternoon
we named the animals, by quarter till four
half had disappeared.
Each tick of the clock has been goodbye.

Open your mouth, poet;
what do the wrens say now
of our comings and our goings?   ✍

Ruffians

Springs winds roll through the house
front to back, west to east, then
join their friends who've run
around the side fleecing pansies,
tormenting shrubs.
God only knows what shenanigans
they'll find on the other end of town.
    I've been rattled (and who hasn't)
by high winds, gaped at black-robed giants
stalking across the plains, sat
with spiders in the dark.

But today they're just enough
to rough you up,
just enough spin to their speech
to keep your feelers sharp.
    I leave the front door open.
Some poems get tossed,
drapes show their legs,
the bell by the window rings—
then out the back and gone,
one gang after another.

Down the block a writer
    refuses to let them in.

He gets his shutters banged,
yard furniture turned upside down.
He gets serious noogies for being a nerd.

"Brace yourself," I tell myself,
"let it go, find the center of chaos."
But it's endless—until it ends.
     The ruffians wear ear buds,
speak in hand jive, show no interest
in form nor esoteric philosophies.
They grab a manuscript on their way through,
     hang it
in the neighbors' trees—
another book launched on the wind.   ✑

SLAMMERS

They have works in progress. They speak
of love. Their school is the stage; they design
their own tests. This is not recess.
There are teachers here.

With maturity that's raised itself
up through the doldrums of repetition
and the dumbing down
of baby boomer naptime, they arrive.

They arrive on the eve of America burning, oil
over the curve, geologic stability and cheap energy
a flicker now, a growth spurt with bills to pay.

They say, Hey, you had a movement back in the day:
Back to the land with flowers in your hair.
Now you look askew at handheld technology,
see selfish singularity. Dig deeper, dude;
there's food in this soil. Our communal garden
is virtual. We meet when and where we please.

We don't fight wars on the street, or, on TV.
We're building a world in the mind.
We rock the mic. There are masters here.
Those Montessori Mommas told our parents,

"Use your words."
Right on, so check this—
language is creation at this game level.   ✒

Memory

The thing with the sky is
the thing with us all—
nothing stays put, it just blows through.
Memories of the round refrigerator and that dog,
the one that barked all night against the wind,
     when recalled and retold
might become a certified *Chupacabra*
and the background song of longing.

The memory of the impression of just moments ago
     is long gone.
The sky in the first line had a fleet of quilted geese
passing overhead. Remember?

My brother and I grew up in the same two story house.
He remembers a secret passage
from attic to basement, lost souls drifting there.

I remember powdered sugar on French Toast
with orange wedges for smiley faces.
Later I fell through the cracks, tumbled
for years in his underworld.

Now that I've placed it on paper
the sky is a seething storm.

It's grown on its own!

But there was one girl who loved me. I'm sure of it.
We told one another the world.

We galloped like horses,
chewed stems of wild sweet grass,
lay on our backs playing hide and go seek
    in transformer clouds, clouds
high and friendly and willing to learn.
They used to be stairways, but I taught them
to be avatars. That's my story.

Memory is a cistern of flowing water
(half submerged changing faces)
and the thing with the sky
    is the thing with us all—
like those pterodactyls in the first line of the poem.   ৰ

BONES IN HER SUNSET
for Joan Logghe

She is the age of my brother if he had lived,
born when presidents wore hats, wrote their names
in my text books, growled over the ways
they would cut up Europe when we got through over there.

I want her for president, settle for sandwiches and soup.
She tells me again how she arrived,
an American triangle completed, open on one end.
Pittsburg to the Pacific to the Rio Grande Uplift.
She is ageless, though I know this can't be so.
She is born again, a few times anyway.

Her husband stacks rocks on top of stories,
comes home to the peaches he has planted.
Some people think he's a local but this
may, in fact, not be his home planet. With him
construction is higher math, conversation is travel.
He pulls a library from his nail bags and you read
blueprints like a star chart. She loves him to death.
Good thing he too has learned to climb
from his own casket. She says her sunset has bones.

Directions to her house include a caveat—
in case of flash flood, come back tomorrow.

She lives on the other side
of near catastrophe, has survived the imprisonments
of cultural lethargy, tunneled through wet sand
with her candle blown out, planted fruit trees,
attracted lightning. There are grand babies.

Touching is not enough. You must read to children,
follow them under the bushes, hold your breath
at the end of the branch, fight like a banshee
for what must be theirs. She holds each of their names
like a moon coming up, tucks them in like the last river.
Water is everywhere on her desert. What pick hasn't struck
dry dirt, true longing gone on a little too long?
Now she's writing love letters.

The old world is a handmade dress, blue dishes,
blood on the rock. She never abandoned temple,
built on top of sand, let the wind be her angels.
She rebuilds the world—as instructed.
She has covered her head in silver, every moment,
then, is a call to prayer.   ✍

ONE STAR TO ANOTHER

All day long they bring me gifts:
refrigerator magnets, catch of the day,
nets of sad seaweed, rows of painted saints,
one act plays, the inevitable limp,
their idea of butterflies.

They bring me plans for world order,
a silver locket with five shy dreams,
a walking mumbling monolith of grievances,
imitations of tigers and utensils,
hilarious comedy—Oh my god.

The bring manuscripts of the lives they thought,
museums of math and devotion,
tribulations, hang nails, beauty,
brilliance, random distractions.
All day long this series of sideshows.

They see me as a king propped up on elbows.
I could add my tired smile to the heap.
When I'm a prince they smell the gold in my pockets,
tug my sleeve all the way down the block.
Inexhaustible, they think.
At first I thought so, too.

I gave them witness in return, a shelf
and jeweled box to hold treasures,
an altar for their precious photographs.
Tomorrow I'm clearing the decks.
My heart already hurts.

They'll rail against the rising ice,
changes in my system.
They'll blame themselves, feel unworthy.
Now their gifts will be torches tossed on cities.

They'll bring statues and stacks of paintings,
but not like before. What doesn't burn
will be dumped in the ocean.
Fires along the road. Fires in the sky.
Gifts of anger everywhere, their backs to me now.
It's not like I can stop watching.

Love doesn't decay, but if I don't grow cold
they'll never turn to face another star.   ✌

HOOK, STITCH AND HALLELUIAH
for my friend passing through the Psych Ward

From here we see
the floating line of Sandia Peak,
her cheek turned to the sky,
but we don't see the hand
that lifts her to the light.

We see the broken crust, the breaking
open and open, birds coming
and going from her parted lips.
We hear their cries
     but we don't know
the full length of their song.

There's a spider at the heart of this story.
Her work is knitting. Diligently
     she repairs
places torn by twisted limbs,
stretched out of shape
by callous deeds, greed,
too many sharp words.

She mends the net
as we toss and turn from scene
to scene, as we wander

close to the edge—
she's dauntless in high wind.

In the silence behind day,
by the light of night,
    she anchors the mind,
picks up every stitch—
her perfect synaptic pattern.

Sometimes, when we step
to the side and let the world
rush busily by,
    we hear her singing,
but we don't know
the full measure of her love;
we've never seen the end
of her thread.   ✍

Expected

The answering machine is a steady "3",
nothing blinking, nothing tugging,
no launch trembling for takeoff,
no plumber on the way.

The trees are leafed. The 'céquia runs.
Fruit flies have found us.

I look for my enemies. Gone.
Bored no doubt with my lack of imagination.
Peace and rapture, even they seem stale.

But the moment is not without breath
and a certain filling.
Someone is finally home from war.

Stories later—
Here, friend, settle in. ❧

Automatic Living

Does it matter which match
I strike first, the line I use?
This is all new, nevertheless,
the sun rises full on, ready or not,
    to see what craziness
we've cooked up in our night dreams.

It's not some part of me that knows,
but this knowing that is neither
noun nor verb, liquid nor gas.
    It's not the ice,
but something after it's gone,
before it came. The beginning, they say,
    is a long ways away.
They're looking for it. Godspeed, I say.

Next door a father holds his daughter
on the shady side of morning,
brushes her forehead,
    becomes the ocean.
Before this, he thought himself singular.

Terrified of the cold we devil worship it,
follow it
    down, down, down

to the end of night.
We'll pierce the sun the same way.
Something here wants to know itself.

He turns and takes her back into the house.
The sun continues to rise.
No one has to tell him
　　how to hold her.
They reach for the spoon together.　✆

Monkness

We're in a monk's moment, a moment
of renunciation. Deny
the sharp and glittery objects,
the temptations of sleep
and long words ending in "ion".
Deny the light.

Renounce the bandits of hate and of love,
any fantasies of oversoul or afterlife.
Burn each house to the ground.

Walk away. Your quest
for the absolute is your arrogance.

This is a monk's moment, and some pauses
being longer than others, this table
stretches back through lifetimes—
but you stopped believing all that.

The cloth here is dull; the stone floor
is worn, dished smooth
but never enough.

A monk's moment is a story unto itself,
a sack of turnips, squeaky prayers—

a personal story with a clock, a tick,
an empty plate and a bomb.
I am not a monk, but my indulgences
are no proof of that.
At first I was fooled by fullness.　᪥

Visiting with a Friend

From the third floor we talk
about the cognoscenti of Cahokia;
the asteroid that stopped dinosaurs in their tracks;
mammoth packets of knowledge, too large
    for language but easily passed
one person to another. We talk
about the flicker of oil, Osage heroes.
We sip words from the cup of evening,
savor conversation's form.

It occurs that if they can manufacture hell,
we must design freedom.
Queens and kings, councils, congresses,
cardinals and intercessors, pharmaceutical
companies and insurance firms
have all agreed on danger as our currency.
We used to subscribe, surrender.

Night travels unnoticed through the trees.
The mountain resting in haze
grants everyone passage.
    The turning is inside.
And something we call safety.
Safety—that rebel thought, that heresy.

We lean against the rail while warm skies
    flower overhead; we rest
in the knowing that passes between us.

The trees here also grow at night.   ❧

ENTERING THE WORLD

I'm pointing to the sinking stone.
If you follow it down
darkness will dilate your heart
like an undersea bloom.

If you follow it down
the sharp cries of dinosaur birds
like an undersea bloom
soften and soften, become friends.

The sharp cries of dinosaur birds
and the breathless depths of night dreams
soften and soften, become friends,
a galaxy cluster of newborn babes.

The breathless depths of night dreams
and you at the center of everything flying out,
a galaxy cluster of newborn babes,
an octopus crawling, cleaning the bottom.

You at the center of everything flying out
blinded by ink flowing from pages,
an octopus crawling, cleaning the bottom,
your bones dissolving, your scaffolds of meaning.

Blinded by ink flowing from pages
you reach for the surface, but the surface is gone,
your bones dissolving, your scaffolds of meaning.
There's nothing, really, you left behind.

You reach for the surface, but the surface is gone;
darkness will dilate your heart.
There's nothing, really, you left behind;
I'm pointing to the sinking stone.   ∽

I Fish
what to do with the dead

Think of me strong for three days,
a moon, a season, whatever
your sundial and ceremony call for.
Hug me to the earth. Tie me
as strips of colored skin
to flutter with the birds.
Pick up a handful of dirt.

I've been more
than a gust of wind, though fleeting
in my own mercurial way.
I've been backed up
in the dream, held for ransom.

My passion moved among the trees
to faces on the street,
rotting leaves, slope of city,
rusty trash barrel and sound
of the onward sea.
No two nights were alike.

You think I have forgotten you
but even our most casual passing
has been an instant of joining,

and once that was done
we face the shore as one.
Sometime we clawed
out each other's eyes.
It's all the same sexy undoing.

Think of me now, all the ways
I limped and failed, muddied
the current, tried to laughed it off.
We work in the field awhile,
then rest our hoe against the rail.
I was a bell ringer—
"Break in the line.
"Storm approaching.
"Everyone, come to the table."
I was an idea of love good as the next.

Thoughts of loss are like a stringer
of fish in the river. Take them home
and eat them, or set them free.
My camp here is cold.
I brushed out my tracks best I could.
When your candle in the window is finished,
I will be complete.   ✍

Remain the Wind

Reveal the earth,
its fallible flowering; steer
our family on a course of thriving,
relieve their toys of war,
replace revenge with water.
Remain the birds.

Remain the dirt paths with hello
in a thousand tongues.
Remain the wind
to inform our spinning, to carry
the word village to village.
Remain the word.
Remain the spinning.

Forgive the last fearful grabbing,
the naked shelters, banking,
hording, monuments.
The only thing pressing
our skin is the wind,
the frontier in between.
Remain the wind.
Remain the giving.

The ones who refuse to see

are the ones who need
to be seen.
See them here. See
how the children step up
after a kind word.
Remain the children.

The seagull has carried us
aloft, to the cliff,
the rain across the plains,
the buffalo
in her breath, the wind
one shore to another—
the music of it all.
Remain the music.
Remain the word.

All that has been done
is recorded
in the layers of the wind.
We bow our heads
to drink in the stream.
The breeze across the water remains.
Remain the birds.
Remain the wind.

Remain the water.
Remain the word. ❧

BIRDNESS

Bloom Aquatic

In the river at eye level
I breath above and below.
I'm on the move.
Birds cry in the faraway. In the river
lines of stars are the trails of our lives,
songs unto themselves. Always,
the underground, the current,
some sky for the sun.

These trees will never leave me, the dirt
never leave me,
the bank with roots, my family
beside me keeping up—trying to keep up.
This could be my story.

My brother dies, stars wobble.
I go over the falls.
I'm long gone. No—
I'm still here. It is they who are gone.
I'm caught on a rock, flat
on my back, cracked in half.
I'm out of water, out of river,
out of place. The clouds are uncertain.

Draw another river, I say.

Draw a river with singers
that go all the way to the sea.
I'm listening to the sun.
    I'm eye level with myself.
I'm high water lifting a body.   ❧

EXTENDED TOUCH

Cut loose and drifting
I stop/start, mythologies within/without.
I flee the human-made, find some dirt
where the fences are down, where
the road empties into salt brush.
I snap back, the engine still running,
panes of painted glass, contracts
made to resemble purpose.
Anyone's idea could be too much.
I'm hovering and I know it.

I think of place and I cry.
Not any place but every place. That place.
If I named the places I love
I would still not be home.
I will say that this is not my planet,

but that's not exactly true.
I'm afraid to talk to a five year old, afraid
of what he will tell me.
I'm afraid I don't know him.
What was it he wanted?
Where was he was going?

I will go somewhere and survive.

I will ask questions under my breath. I will bloom
until exhausted. I'm outside in the dirt.
I'm small with a round face;
I'm as big as the neighborhood.
I know so much.
What I know may be of little use.
Someone is placing a gentle hand at my back.

A Lifetime that Counts

I, for one, could have been the man
to bear down on those thugs
with blazing lead—but I wasn't.

I could have given the orders
on a thousand mornings to entertain
the poor with the crack of gallows;
could have looked them all in the eye
and wiped my knife on their sleeves.
I was there—but I didn't.

I watched the red train, headlong, full speed,
derail into the unsuspecting city.
I am not a dove nor innocent whisper.
I could have been the one
to pull that switch, could have
punished them by taking their children.
I could have worn the other mask.

I could have looked the other way—
so many big cars to drive, bills to fill. Anyway,
who has time outside of television?
I could have slept in the cellar
season after season, so much dust on sagging glass.
I could have pretended to pray

when I covered my head.
I could have pulled the trigger on my brother
over and over, but I refrained.

Finally—a lifetime that counts. &

I Didn't Tell Him Stories

Before he pushed the music away
he was pennies on the rails, he was fireflies in the woods,
his hands were mulberry stained, he was caught like a bug.
He was my father, but not yet.

His own father was God, his mother an invalid.
His younger brother never forgave him.
I was a younger brother once.

He pointed out the house where he was raised—
trolleys gone, streets paved.
Two wars later my friends rented that house,
painted the walls into wonderland.
We dropped Acid there.
Donovan Leitch sang "Guinevere" and "The Fat Angel".
It was close as rain... it was far, far away.

He was at the top of his class, hell in the boxing ring.
He lost a bet and shaved his moustache.
My father found alcohol before I did.
His fraternity was XXX with a hand across a skull, a piercing ruby eye.
When I got busted for drugs he silently cringed.

Back then we had to cross the desert at night.
We sat together in different dark.

I was difficult, too.
When I asked him about boys he said,
I can't help you there. And that was the easy stuff.

He was storied and well spoken, a gentleman
tipping his hat, a ladies' man, up to a point.
He taught me to think, then he taught me to walk.
I didn't stick around to tell him my story.
We both had thunder in our blood.

He was a lake trout under two feet of ice.
He was impossible.
He was more beautiful than they knew.
He was my father, then.
The music went on without him.   ⋘

QUIBBLE

Before we get caught up
in table-banging and touché
let me just say, No—
which is a complete sentence.
You're tugging my sleeve and telling me
you can find a better deal.
You want product; you want fame, deliverance.
You're pulling my leg.
I make my living giving away
pieces of me. I've gone over the falls
more times than I can count.
Throw your money on the bed or call a cab.

No, I will not quibble.
No, you cannot pay for the kindness.
The overhead projection
of how we fit together is a sky
I can no longer fly through.
Rent's due.
Soft talk with big floppy ears
is the sock puppet I made of myself.

Strike line twelve—
I've called a cab for myself. Like I said,
I'll only miss part of you. ❧

BIRDNESS

Everyone has a road that receives their feet,
a secret side street, a grandfather tree
or sloping hill that says, Friend, I see you.
Someone has been watching.
Not the someone who officiates downtown
nor the ones who signed on the parent line,
but a *friendly other.*

You tested the ice with your foot,
ran into the middle flapping your arms.
You pretended to fly, then, pretended you couldn't.

Decisions had to be made:
    this is how I will survive;
    this is how far I can trust;
    this, this quirky footwork is how
I will wend my way through the world.

You figured it out before you could speak.
And they thought you were helpless.
Either a monster tried to snuff you
or you're crazy—and that's a dilemma.
All you have are your feelings now.
You must trust your birdness,
stop pretending not to have wings.   ∾

ARC OF OUR WATER

There is a line that returns
with a village attached
    but it's not the cord
I've been casting.

Whip of stick, snap of tongue,
brick to throat, foot on head.

When the craft of my cutting
collapses and I tire
of muscling up on others,
    the power I thought I held
leaves me—abandoned.
Where is my town now?

Where is *my enough,*
my logical admirers, a patsy
    to pay the price, the skill to juggle
these hot potatoes of shame?

No one comes forward so I lay and wait

with social worker words, arguments
tight as dissertations, verses
that come with a halo.

If blame is a bully, vengeance is a stalker.
Under my bed: a baseball bat.

Is this my king sized bed, my weeping
walls and tsunami credit card;
    is this my clutching,
my postponement?

Through the rain I think I hear
the sun, shining—I hear
    children's voices,
soup simmering around family fires, men
taking turns bandaging one another, women
taking turns counting out the saplings.

Is this my village arrived without punishment?
    Is this my place
in the field, a woman handing me a plate
to share the melon?
Is this the arc of our water?   ؘ

Friends from Long Ago

This window has no worlds beyond it.
This window wants what's coming to it.
At the appointed time this window
will open to reveal the unimaginable.

We left the cave with its rug door, crossed the valley
to rendezvous with those who'd taken the long way around.
We're companions meeting other companions. We're on our way.
Up here, one hero's as good as the next.

When we were friends
we became enemies. Those two words
meant so much and windows went
every which way then. We shot off
like sparks into the disappearing wind.
Who's to say which is the long way around.

We'll meet again, but not
the again we left behind. Yes,
the letters stopped but not the rotation
of light nor need for bread.
I thought I should return.
I thought you held the place of home.
But you, too, have a crossing to make.
On every rocky coast a window with a light.   ◈

KIND OF A COWBOY THING

With my old straw on the dash
and untold miles to go,
I've already told the rebels
how to find this road.

Smoke blows down south
but is working its way north. It works
its way with machetes, with dynamite,
with quick deeds and prevailing winds.

The North is also closing in. Soon,
we'll park these machines like so many
see-through singlewides bleached in the sun.
How long's it been since you and I ran off the road?

In the days of roadside miracles,
we offered Apache Tears
to the river of new beginnings.
Mountain water tumbled that marriage

toward good completions—in a hurry.
I tried to hold the moment
before it finished by blaming our friends.
I wanted something to be broken.

Fault, even mine, seemed better
than unexplained goodbye.
I'm walking and I'm talking—out here
the horizon is everywhere, then disappears. ❧

ROUNDNESS

The cup is not round, the earth
not perfectly round, this cycle of forgiveness,
    those African moments.
In the courtyard, in the dirt,
shortly before sunset, the marimbas
were arranged under fragrant trees.
A string of colored lights.

The show began with Venus introduced
by sliding clouds. A rustle of children
passed in small thunder
with a lighted hoop. The music
shifted one-thirty-second then
resumed its shape. Music is almost,
but not quite, round.

I did not return to the same Oklahoma.
My parents, dead so many years,
keep changing, growing older or younger,
showing their stripes, their out-of-roundness
that had nothing to do with me.

Plume is a pretty word so I will say
a *belch* of smoke above Mogollon Rim
is sending sparks and cinders blasting

into the jet stream. Just like Krakatau
the smoke will find its own tail,
complete the circle.
      A forest fire is sometimes round.
But shovels are not round, flight patterns,
canisters, instructions for refueling,
cries of animals caught in the blaze.

Every time I come back you say, hey,
where've you been. We both know
it's not a real circle, but it's close enough.
What looked like dismissal was really
another invitation. We show up again.
No, it was not perfect then.

It will spin until it wobbles.

After all this time we've learned to turn and turn
away from the roaring wind,
and that is part of the roundness.   ⊸

CLEAN THUNDER

It's time to clean the altar.
It's sometime after, the days
hotter but shorter. On the grasslands
the dancing has begun: ankle bells,
feathers falling for veterans.
You are all invited.

It's time to replace reverence
with honor. It is God
who will stand and listen.
It was one lie after another:
I was strong—not.
I was weak—not.
I was innocent—not.
I deserved what I got—not.

I wanted us all to be greater
than we were, and I will
burn this body
as many times as it takes.
I will replace those lies with thunder.

Thunder rolling in the black and green.
Thunder coming up
through my feet, in my speech,

the air trembling with truth.

The stone was washed in blood.
I have scrubbed and scrubbed.
Enough!

My heart breaks, multiplies.
I command the wind
and all the ashes are carried away.

In the emptiness I swing my axe.
My altar is not the fallen earth.
There is no blood on this blade. ᕔ

WAVES
song of the empath

The wolf passes through me
on its way to the wind. The wind
passes everyone, makes love
in reckless forward motion, runs

circles in the lagoon where
you thought it couldn't go.
What passes for purpose is ordered chance,
some ideas better than others: turtles,
tectonics, photosynthesis.

Laurie peddles her bike along the shore.
She's past counting calories
and false windows in the church.
The evening is luminescent turquoise to blue-black.
All is silhouette—
one winged palm after another.

The outgoing tide makes me
dig my feet into sand, the breeze
lulls, changes direction.
Laurie waves—passes through me.   ⊷

SONG SEARCH

This is a song without moon,
a crooked road toward rendezvous.
It's the night I arrived and
angels swooped closer for a look.
There's possibility here.

I say nothing without those
who have gone before: beats, beats
with Moloch on their minds,
a cotton picker trying to walk the line,
the silence of a fallin' star.
I say nothing

and mean a broken city looking for its heart.
I think open pit mines, field hollers,
horse hoof Jell-O. I mean
     to think something pretty, and I do,
but not all the time.
I'm just saying, it's a sword with a backlash.

I put my hands on every wheel I can.
I use my body inside out, outside in.
Swoop closer, angels, it's my turn for a look.

It's angels in heat; it's cold tempered steel;

it cuts like a diamond when it's real.
Yesterday I saw two halves
walking toward me. This morning
   nobody resembles themselves.
And there's a lot more that's none of my business.
I lied—there's a moon in every song.

Keep looking, angels, I'm here somewhere.   ⤜

Just Keep Walking

It takes a long time to walk
through that town. They have sirens
of their own and ways of making laundry.
The sign says, No Hitch Hiking, Out Of Town By Dark,
but nights turn into black and whites,
years in the making.
It's an epic with jump cuts,
a house of mirrors, sidewalks that heave.
Just keep walking.

If I hadn't already been hurting, caught
in a southern story, I'd have seen it coming.
I'd have rented a Plymouth.
I'd have seen the cardboard.
But they didn't make up that town just for me.

There's a kind of outlaw
that's not an outlaw at all—
they'll hurt anybody's children, laugh
at guilt and the unavoidable trouble of others.
They do it in black leather but
mostly they do it in suits and heels.
All their teeth are gold.
I wish I could've walk a little faster.

A tumbleweed landed against my leg, said
"There's shade down by the river."
That's the best way to get your mail on the road
without it being pilfered.
There's good information on that wind.

At the other end of town
there's a check point with reasonable attorneys,
justified housewives, the outraged
and the bitterly correct.
Your dissertation is not what you hold—
but your hand.

At the other end of town
you saw them then,
playing popup store fronts, wars,
courts, calibrations. They winced
at the light from your palm.
You're over the line but the road goes on.
It took a long time
to walk through that town.   ᔑ

WHO CHOOSES WHOM

I find you again but not
by way of the smoking red altar
nor revelatory mountain.
Something more along the line
(or the un-line) of a wave.

When I was younger I chose things,
and back then the day was work,
    and I was the one being worked.
At night we rode out ahead.

I set upon a course
of *this* or *that*, a branching river,
    active exploration.
The fingers of the world were worms.
I admit to everything.

My friend doesn't know where
    her body is in space.
She bumps into tables, spills the beans.
She's mad at someone. Us and them.
This isn't happening, she says.

I admit it now—everything is real.

The trees have eyes. The stone walk
and metal gate; the table, its legs;
books, moisture, voices in rooms;
the smell of garlic and diesel—
all have eyes. The space between.

I didn't find you by design this time.
I didn't *do* anything.   ⸙

EVEN WITH THE SUN TURNED ON

Day Dreaming, My Job

By myself at a table without
stir of synapse, first line or arrow
aiming into the imaginarium.
    Nothing has happened
and no movement from which
observers can make reference, conclusion.

Journal, books, notebook, pen,
all suspended and untouched.
Eyes adrift slowly rest
no place near, then travel on.
    A pair of blue gypsy doves
from belfry to vanishing.

I'm working, I say.

And they pass me over
because I wear the sandwich board
of a writer. Suspect, no doubt
without device or additional apps.
Notebook open all morning,
    this empty page repels
even the most courageous,
the pungent shield of a juniper insuring
    that nothing else grows

within its blank stare.

But listen—the crunch
of silica and slurping of groundwater
as roots drive and drink
their story into the earth.
  Civilizations pass by: homes
of packrats and beetles, bones of the loving
and forgotten, Comanche camps,
refuse dump of Clovis Man,
microbes with lives of conquest
and wonder. Phantoms!

Now, they exclaim,
abandon everything above this line—
all is mere scaffolding up 'til now.

All in good time, I say—
  I'm working. ✍

PLAYING TRAIN

One good thing about the sky
is that it lets you see out.
You don't know when the sun
might change its mind
but for now it's a relationship
with boundaries and plans for college.
You can see that.

Last Christmas the adults
dug out an old train, steel wooled
the tracks, puzzled the pieces.
Once the engine got past growling
sparks threatened the grass carpet,
called for action without elections.
You were on the crew,
kept boxcars on the rails.

After fifty years that urge
to blow it all up was still there.
"Time for dinner" meant destroy
the infrastructure, infantry, scientists, civilians.
"It must be a 'boy thing'," she said.

Creation, Preservation, Destruction.
That's the kind of sun that shines here.

This time it's your turn to keep it
on track, put out fires.
Graduation might look like setting the table,
feeding the children.
Rain or shine, this train goes in a circle.
You can see that.　❧

SNAP BEANS

I want you
to read me that poem in bed
I want you to
read me *all* your poems
in bed do as I say

Hear my voice
close to your ear
carve me
give me
your stories on the sheet

I am salt
coming to you
I am snapping in two
you think you're safe
three hundred and eighty miles away Ha

Kill me poet with everything you've got   ✦

At the New Mexico Arts and Crafts Show

She speaks of process with each artist,
learns how to paint a "resist"
on silk, on clay, on glass,
how to apply the wax
to stop yellow at blue.

She rules out the things
that may not be true,
sets aside as holy the absolute leaf,
the Chinese character
for double happiness.

This one is a farmhouse
paddling against autumn chamisa;
this one a talismanic urge, and this
an *ofrenda* of squash and fruit
for the happy dead.

On a bench in the center
they rest with strawberries,
paint with words between them.
She eyes optimism with caution,
plunges toward purple and orange. ✧

Boy

I've decide again to be a boy.
It was easier after playing dress up for a few minutes.
After all, there's nothing wrong
with thrusting and boosting,
with poking the ground to plant the corn,
with piercing the sky, making roads
by walking to the village of my sweetheart.

There's plenty wrong with stealing children,
and it's downright evil to say, "Pro Choice"
then vote for dropping bombs.
     But it's a team effort.
Haven't we arrived together?

A single cell grows toes, wiggles
onto the Savannah. We've been upright
since before we left Ethiopia.
What I know is: I've decide to be a boy.
I'll be a boy with the wolf in my nose.
I'll be a boy with mud for war paint.
     I'll be a boy dancing
with my wanker in my hand.
I'll read you poetry all the way down.

I'll be a boy whether my mother

likes it or not. I may not be the boy
my father wants. I can pitch
and I can catch. I'm a major league boy.
I'm a boy that knows the ropes, a flower
    that catches its pray.
I'm no longer afraid that I'll hurt you.
I know how to step aside.

That "sissy" thing is twisted.
An open-hearted male is
an awesome power to behold.
I'm a boy; thank you.

I'm a boy making trouble,
a dust cloud in the afternoon.
I'm a boy holding you tender against the cold.
    I'm upright on the earth
and I'm thinking ahead. I'm walking
with a beautiful woman inside.

I'm naked—streaks of mud on my face.
    I'm dancing
with the seeds in my hand.   ⬿

SKATE

The cloudiness I could not outrun,
drone of the tired but tireless city,
some aggressive squeaking in the trees
that sounds like insects
but in fact is probably hummingbirds.

I ran completely out of coffee yesterday,
and to the shock and dismay
of my spiritual and forwardly abundant friends
I say that I have 52 cents to last the rest of my life.

If they stone me for uttering new age heresy
you can giggle over my remains
in a government plot (sorry) in the South Valley.

I feel a little better as I begin thinking
about that really cute Swiss girl
from the reading on Sunday at Acéquia Booksellers,
the one who loves to feel tall in roller skates
and has danced on quad wheels in Central Park
with men whose names she never asked.
I'm a disaster on skates.

So I imagine sitting at a little 2-up
near the concessions scribbling hummingbird poems

that look like high-ceilinged mosques
but are really about sex.
I imagine the delight in her eyes
as she goes round and round all laced up,
then I take her home and we find ways
for her to be as tall as she wants.

And now I remember that I have a five dollar voucher
for a local coffeehouse—and her phone number.
There is a break in the clouds.
I could do this town on wheels.   ⋘

PUDDLES

Miles and miles of hybrid corn
    and the posture of wooden pews
        raised you upright.

The near straight line
    of that horizon gives me something
        to push against. The pure blue above it

comes out of nowhere, keeps expanding.
    It's an open space
        where we could brush wings,

circle in whimsy,
    find rain puddles on the desert
        reflecting rapture. I'm falling

toward one now
    but I'm not wounded,
        just a little breathless.   ❧

GET A (GALAXY) MOTEL

Stars rappel the vertical peak,
    trace the face of Cabezon.
        A crescent moon on the desert is enough

to find your lover.
    Leaned up against a car
        we find Saturn, three star clusters

and a planetary nebula, faint but busy,
    making babies before falling
        into ruffles of dark horizon.

The only question mark is a constellation,
    the arc of procreation everywhere.
        As far as stars go

our sun is in a minority—
    no push and pull love cluster,
        no threesome, not even

a binary partner to swing with;
    every day she rises and sets by herself.
        And that lonely star stuff, baby,

is what we're made of—no wonder
    the night sky makes us
        want to have sex with everyone.   ❧

No Thanx

A young woman tears through my apartments,
knocking on doors, running from a pickup, a man
circling the block. She's looking
for a phone to call her mom.
She has a plastic bag full of plastic curlers.
She is hot and out of breath.
She is not about her tattoos. She is
about nine years old. She works
as a dancer so she's got be at least eighteen.

I insist she drink water.
She catches up with herself
a city block and a gasp at a time.
"You're safe now.
"You're going to be okay.
"You're already okay." She folds
like a Bedouin tent on my floor.
Her mom will meet her on the street.

For a moment I'm the good daddy—
as if she might know what that looks like,
as if everyone carries that picture with them
even if they ripped it off the Internet.
Another drink of water. Then
her training kicks in and she turns

like a kitten toward my caring, expecting
the next scene to be sex.
Isn't that how a girl should say thanx?   ⋖

VENDY

I imagine her on a slope of sand
with her domesticated coyote and defiant garden,
tucking words into her back pocket
for late night retrieval. I imagine her swooning
for all that the morning brings.

I see myself there, but not enough
to shift the wind
or cause disruption in the rhythm
of husband, children, further horticulture.
My wanting would be grasshoppers.

Listen, I say to them,
leave her garden alone—
her rhyming rows and clumps
of Olde English herbs, Chinese wings,
that butterfly bush.

Leave her swooning as she once did
in the safety of a crowded circle,
books at our feet, personal myths,
an astronomer's blessing.
What's to have and to hold; what better way

than to start the day with a secret that's open?

On the west side where the sun
comes up twenty eight minutes later
I imagine her small moist hand touching
the sharp dark nose of a coyote, a kind word

throwing light into the canyons of Utah.
I imagine the cool earth of my den.   ⋖

THE MORNING TO WHICH I'M WAKING

Wet hair, red energy drink,
personal journal on her lap,
she sits facing morning's sun.

Doves hoot unseen while Sunday traffic
starts up in small gusts.
My balcony is now a foreign country.

She has brought the sea,
the pale setting moon,
a bouquet of lilac rain—

these things permeate my house.
I have my reasons
for waiting so long

but they no longer seem important.
My bookcase is double stacked,
crammed with must and journals.

New articles lie on the floor:
her boots, cranberry socks, bra.
When I let go of the story

of how I got here
I recognize those city doves.
How long have they been calling? ❧

COUNTING ONE ANOTHER

Death will be a morning, she says.
But I'm in one presently
and God is flying in from nowhere.
An open door, oil on the streets,
birds and the new word for bebop.

God has been arriving since 7:14 a.m.
Every flight is a journey into now.
The worst pain is believing a lie.

I die. I died. I will have died.
Now God is a growl lifting a dumpster
with two steel fingers, spent petals
fluttering. I flourish.
I will have flourished.
I become the bird of my choosing.

Or say someone comes into your life
and you run either to or from them.
You are layered, full of portent, grace,
the only now there is. Truly

there are no two hands alike,
but this morning I can only recall
three or four hands ago. Mary,

Julieanne, that man at the meeting.
And my own hand should count.

How we fumble to find one another
even with the sun turned on.　❧

Together in the Wind

The way she spoke of wind
I knew I would have to accept it as another,
other lover, invisible friend,
unknown constellation beyond the equator.
From the East—a mild fifteen.
Perhaps it was the mountain
that turned it, curled it under
and back over the foothills, gentle,
slightly cooler than summer's pulse.

Above the pale stone range and leaning out
the marine fossil of a cloud, flat
and wide with curved spine bloomed
in the emptiness, bloomed
as we all do from nothing, stars
coming and going through its fins.

The wind teased at her skirt,
her hair, her thoughts
running out across the desert, the sea, the ice.
She was the blonde rock upon which she sat.

If I was to say if it were the land
that held her, or she embracing it,
I would point to the red crescent moon

slipping like a stick
into the firework haze of the city
as it sailed west to become east, rinsed
and white over the vast Pacific.

The language of how a thing becomes
its opposite is spoken here, going
to the end always a beginning.
I know there are stronger winds than these.
The unseen friend feels different
on different skin. Wind
parts us like grass, brings us close
beneath this unfathomable spread of stars. ✒

How It Comes

Some days I seem to only see the falling:
the leaf as it lets go, rain
running down the ruined street,
the land spent, maybe forgiven.
So much has been cut and fit
and is already on its way home.
But what really is finished, what
soft wing or sharp tongue
was ever the season itself?

The going always goes—the eyes burn out,
the broom sweeps by, skeletons
twist erotic in sea-bound currents.
But what of the coming—and from nothing!

I follow it down, a cat after a bug.
From a fallen log an exhale
of unseen moisture rises like a wish;
a cooling breeze considers its breath;
no one yet thinks: *thunderhead.*

Dust drifts through incalculable ages,
collects on a window sill of its own making,
shouts as a new born star. Dust becoming.

Deep in mind there's a nuance of thought,
a dream fragment like the edge
against which something will move.
Later, the color-hint of a feeling.
No language yet—just this arriving.
Tomorrow: the invention of a world. ॐ

It's About the Vibe

It's not any quieter here
than it was in my dreams—

between buildings the plaintive meow
of that fat tabby, drone of lawn machines, a jet
nearing then fading in swells.

An unseen bird is working at something:
a rhythm chiseling, a sculpture
forming in my spine, my stomach.
This body, this studio.

Underneath the work of the wind, I feel
the pipes in the walls,
distant surge of the Interstate,
    that repetitive phrase
I've often called longing and
up till now had claimed as my own.

A car stereo rocks it
like a garbage truck dropped in a pond.
Oh, how we soothe ourselves.

And now it's my turn:
the scratch of gel pen on paper,

thumping of my bare feet registering
    a small gust of emotion,
a deeper breath letting the moment go.

How far will they travel, how long?
All this broadcasting. Collision.
Is that you I hear turning the page?   ✍

SAYS OWL

I'm trying to see my way through
    the night and the night
        pretends to be elsewhere.

Go blind, says owl,
    blind as a root.
        I have grown in sunlight

but even more in darkness.
    If I speak of melons and sea foam
        and detectives it's because my Mexico

has a jaguar's tongue and my love
    lives in a house I've never seen.
        It perches on the edge of a village

we build together
    when birds blink to sleep.
        She is walking in the next street.

If I have passed her without knowing
    then I must learn to walk
        with my eyes closed. ❧

THE PAPER WORK OF POETRY

I'm an artist in heat.
The moon is one day past full.
There are formulas.
Shower before coffee; poetry before email;
kindness first; closure when possible.

The moon is melancholy; the moon
is indifferent; the dark side shifts;
the far side remains; the moon
is largely in my mind. What,
after all, is speculation?

In an impromptu world we engage
    with intention then see
if the next random emergence
is the avatar's voice.

We are artists—not formulas.
    We are the heat we seek.
When I get through filling out this report
I will return
    to take my place
in the dream chamber beside you.   ✒

ACORNS FOR THE DEER

How I Got Here

I came by way of the gold plated oilman,
the doctor's Oxford cloth, the crust
circumcised from white bread.

Window air conditioners dripped
and lunged through sultry nights.
I came from black and white,

crossed the tracks to hear the jazz.
I was blacklisted at five years old
when I finally opened my mouth.

I came through states where time
stood still, but I didn't know it then.
The fastest thing in town was a

two-door Mercury and a blue crawdad. ✍

LEADVILLE: A FIRESIDE SKETCH

They drill holes in rock ahead
of dynamite, come home
to empty washtubs, wind whistling
down their backs. Most of them
don't know a photograph.

Somebody's walls are banging;
somebody's door is burning. All night
the silver sleeps and the mice move in.

It's a vein and a lode one finger at a time.
It's about 5:00 A.M.
and the cooks are striking matches.
They elbow one another in the gut
and ring their hammers senseless.
They won't need the women 'til winter.

In a matter of hours a man can holler
down the pot-holed valley.
Before he's done he's gray
as a flake. You can trace
his ashes for three generations.

We scratch in the earth; everybody
has dirt beneath their nails.

We slap sticks into a pile, then
that blue snake of wind comes along.

The trains bring them up. Lanterns
swing on pickets, even the boys
are bankers in their dreams,
but don't think the women
aren't looking to get rich.
They'll turn to the men come spring.

It's not *what* you make,
but the *making* what makes
the light shine in the tunnel.
Digging's just what we do;
our whiskers twitch to feel.
It's 5:18—cakes on the griddle.   &

HOMESTEAD

for Cathie O'Connor

Up Old Woman's Creek she sets traps
for gophers, remembers to turn the inverter on
before running water into the garden,
picks bugs from kale.
Behind a wall of double pane windows she grows
pineapples, bananas, heirloom tomatoes.
Forty feet out—the high desert begins.
Maybe it's time for a run to the city.

The bare-dirt towns of prairie dogs
pop up over night, subdivisions that claim
the earth then give it to the wind—
thousands of them now, a specie
gathering in numbers for the drought.
A lanky coyote with sagging teats
is saving her strength for a raid at dawn.
Did I mention the wind?

Up Old Woman's Creek she reads books
made of paper and glue, keeps things
in jars, blows out the candles,
lays awake with the world racing in her mind:
    I think there's enough flagstone to finish the floor.
    Is that mice I hear in the straw bales?

Her man's a doctor of Chinese medicine.
Her man's a monk and brown
from the sun. Her man's becoming
the last gnarly juniper on the hill.
In fifteen years he's only left the valley once.
They take turns leaving the burner on.

She tells herself there's an end to the wind.
But that's only true if you cut life
into seasons, and even then
it rises from the loss
of mornings left behind, from the longing
to touch the smooth wood between us,
the desire to be blown clean.

Up Old Woman's Creek artesian water
tries to hide as long as it can.
It doesn't help to go inside.
She married the land and brought him with her,
but neither can hold her strong enough
to keep her feet in the ground.
Did I mention. . . the wind? ༄

Museums of the West

"Hurrah boys, we've got them!
We'll finish them up and then go home to our station."
—Reported words of George Armstrong Custer at the
outset of the Battle of Little Bighorn

Grave markers in the foreground,
deerskin lodges on the horizon,
deep grass leaning in the breeze.
I want to believe the green of it,
walk across the summer of it
using lightning for my strides.
I'm listening for the children.

The 3 x 5 postcard is peaceful, the Battle
of Little Bighorn done.
I know hundreds of households,
and as many taverns,
where I can find reenactments, lead poisoning.
Conquest, conquest, conquest.

On the battle field I can say words:
past history, shame, forgive.
On the battle field there is honor.

Moving on means leaving the battle,

moving into what has come after.
We are standing in a museum.
This grass has been planted.

On the other side of the tee-pees
there are towns where life is moving.
If you haven't come with fresh meat
and good water—turn around. ᔑ

Delivery to Lakota

What you can see
from a grass mountain a ghost hawk knows
with its eyes closed.

Across the sand hills the ocean
is undeniable. You think you know
where the sky ought to be; you say,
These are my feet flat on the ground.
That's when you fall
    into the mountain,
a beaded trail appearing overhead.

I was dizzy there until a woman
sat me at her table,
put a bowl of soup under my nose.
When the men came home
they showed me the healing lodge
    where ropes are untied
in darkness, darkness is lifted,
brothers turn away from demons and drink.

There's a right way to put fire and water together.

The lava rocks I brought knew their way
up and onto earth's surface.

I found them waiting to help—
agents of renewal and remembering.
    They bring the men back
to their senses, back to the table.
I was a delivery boy from Colorado.
We've got volcanoes
we don't even know how to use.   ✑

Red Bow Blues

We set off smoke alarms with ceremony in hotels.
We were a Pow-wow highway, we were
cases of Pepsi, Pendletons,
Bitter Root, Black Mountain Singers.
  Your friend, the Buffalo.
We'd all come from out there.

I was learning the songs, how to
pass the pipe, hold my tongue.
I was more Anglo Saxon than I'd ever been.
I was peeling off stories, skin.
Everything began happening in circles.

You handed me a small round stone.
Michael told me that if I ever wanted
to talk to you—that's how.

You're a legend of the highway,
a dancer, an F.B.I. casualty.
That year my altar filled with wings.
I never called you on that stone.
Eventually, I gave it to the fire.
By Fall we'd both fallen down.

Your ghosts, my ghosts, so much evil

sneaking around in the sagebrush at night.
So many habits that wouldn't fly free
      on the fourth day.
This drinking thing. This family thing.
These obligations. History
dead, but not properly buried.

At the welfare office in Taos I nodded.
I didn't want you to see me seeing you.
      It's a shame.
It's a God damned shame factory.
My people handing out handouts.
I was—I was not—one of them.
I needed food. Your wife and toddler
needed food. I tried to read magazines.

I could have tossed you that stone
across the waiting room.
Buddy, I could have said,
      this is not our skin.
This is not a real circle.
Next year you'll make the journey.
A piece of hospital paper will say:
      cirrhosis of the liver.
I will say, Travel well my friend.

The stone cracks; the water flies.
I will learn the meaning of these songs.   ✑

Up Abiquiu Way

> "The eyes of the dead somewhere above ground beyond
> shadow still burn like embers and remember the night."
> —John Macker

It's either the edge of escape
or the long circuitous route of a scorpion
looking for a wall to back up against.
It's neither here nor there.
A star rides close to the line,
ducks below the horizon, chances
a few hours in the open sky.
Nobody pays serious attention.

Attempts on your life are numbered
from one to twenty two and a half
and those brick-red rocks go down
two hundred and twenty million years,
but only in geology books.
The land here heaves just fine
without anyone counting, besides,
the stars breathe too fast or too slow
to be heard at a distance.
It's coyote's call.

Even in the middle of the day, you hear them—

Ute, Apache, Diné.
Restless in gushing blood, restless
for murdered land, for stolen children. Restless!
And you don't even own a gun.

But at night you reach for something
when those floor planks creak and shadows
sneak across the *llano* from one fence line to another.
You bolt up straight, wet covers in a knot,
"Take all my cows, take my books,"
but they're not interested—
not in that kind of *sangre*.

Before the waters rose
an artist found the bones of a thousand
government-slaughtered horses,
painted the sky through their hips,
and the Tiger took over the courthouse
in the name of a holy raid. Victims tossed
on top of one another.
I mean it,
there's nobody out here with clean hands.

That's not a stack of red bricks;
that's the earth soaked in spilled blood,
the disenchantment of a hangover.
To the conquerors, everything's a museum—
including that *Indian Room.*

And a scratchy sound is something crawling
across your mind with a stinger aloft.
You can leave the mesa now, but
there's no easy way back down in the dark.
What you know about the taking of slaves
is a slab of your own red meat.
If it's guilt you're trying to hide,
those ghosts will just keep circling.   ⋖

Good Find

I find the tribe I was looking for.
They're still dancing
but don't know, or

pretend not to notice,
that the drumming has stopped.
Their feet are all there

and the dust is down.
Either cicadas or the sound of expansion.
An elder holds the rattle

or I mean to say nothing,
I mean nothing you can photograph.
Their feet are all there,

still dancing. I take up the drum.
My arm is tired.
Pretend not to notice.

We go on that way,
cicadas or the sound of expansion.
I find the drum I was meant for.   &

Good Water Comes

On the other side of the divide,
Coeur d'Alene or Wenatchee,
I rode the rain down to the river.

I was an orchard without a moon,
a reservation of plutonium,
a slope of tansy ragweed on the rise.
I was one flew over the cuckoo's nest
on my way out to sea.

I wrote it all down and I cried it all out.
When that was done
I made a tiny boat of paper-thin bark
and placed my past on the river.
I probably lit a candle, probably
looked up into whatever sky
was there to receive me.

Last night I looked for a raincoat;
I mean a *sou'wester*,
more rubber than fashion, a grip
to hit the deck, fog horn down the night.
I was bracing myself for the news;
    I was weary of the world's truth.

I am my own Jesus, and you are yours.

The smell of good water comes
from sheets cascading granite faces,
chilled sprinkles splashing
on an open sill, children dashing,
    you and me snuggling
three wet afternoons in a row.

I'm a dog-eared book, empty as a stone.
I'm taking my time heading to the coast.
    We make a small fire
as it falls all around us.
The ocean will find us soon enough.   ∾

ACORNS FOR THE DEER

All my neighbor wants to do
is keep those English hogs
our of her garden, leave

some acorns for the deer.
She refuses to move
into Prayer Town, refuses

the healthcare that becomes debt.
She is of the First Light
and gives thanks for that rising.

She owns nothing.
She will have lobster and strawberries for lunch,
clams with currants for dinner.

This may be her last good meal.
Every month more ships arrive—
English, French, Dutch, metal,

cotton, guilt. Who sells the earth?
She is of the land, and when she says
the word *land* she names herself.

She is not for sale.

The newcomers sleep with their animals,
never bathe. They "Cleanse the way"

with pox and bullets—whole villages.
Tomorrow she will bury her children
without knowing they were sinners. ❧

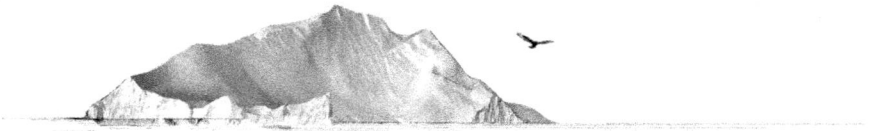

Traffic Always Traffic

Tsunami Now

There's been an earthquake of the heart.
It's rattled dishes all the way
to Sweden; you feel it
circling the world in great waves,
tremors of sadness. Chaos.

We think Japan would know better
than to play with atomics.
We think Britain and America
would be sick of petroleum by now.
We think we know in our hearts
what this shaking can reveal.

I turn to my water,
this cup so willing to help.
I turn in my dream—everything disappears.

Everything, but this quaking.   ✍

LOOK, THERE

Hiroshima—charred meat
on brittle sticks, shadows
still sitting on steps.
After the blast, black rain
rinses the sky
of radiating death.
    But ignore thirst;
this water's not safe to drink.

In the middle of the day
sudden darkness. The sunset
inside glows with poison.
Your hair drops in clumps.
Your body oozes pus.
This, they say,
    will be the end of war, this
heretofore unleashed horror.

In Vietnam the U.S. fought
"a limited war," 400 times
that of the Atomic Bomb.
How far back to the stone age
    would you like to go?
Next time London, Houston,
Albuquerque. Next strike—

the finish of human time.

Who will grow up
in this world; who
will wake from this repetition?
I have no need for so-called facts.
The shadows of Nagasaki
    and Baghdad return
in the eyes of newborns.
Look there for your orders.   ⹊

DROUGHTLAND

In a large and now crowded house with death
at both ends the children have gotten bigger
and moved to the edges.
The weather vane is broken, rattling.
The wind will find its tallness.
They're trying to stay ahead of the rain.

Old people suck moisture from ice trays. No one
has bothered to bring them their teeth.
An honest outlaw will know what I mean.
The real thieves will never read this.
Put your voices together. Everyone
lift your hands to the earth.

There were rivers once, great beings.
It's against the law, you know,
to catch water from your roof.
The truth doesn't need legislation.
They try to outrun the rain, steal it, but can't
swallow a drop. Let's meet on any street.

This house is made of moldy bread
and will dissolve in water.
There is no word nor symbol suitable now;
human dignity is not a brand.

We'll grieve and sing on the road as we've always done,
plastic toys and shutters floating.
The rain will have its day, then move on. ॐ

Mary Ann Ships Out

Meet me on the hill behind the factory,
the dirty stacks, the place where the metal used to grind.
Bring your lipstick, your polka dot dress,
your ticket to Ft. Bliss. This, is our last kiss.

It's your turn to go to war.

You're nervous going down, but it doesn't get any better
in uniform. Lock it, load it, let me straighten your cap.
Like always, we've waited for each other.
Like always, we haven't

Toss your babies to me through the window.
I tear my clothes and count on nothing.
I make trash fires in the freight yard and teach
the history of the rails. I'm feeding the kids first.

We play your videos on the side of an oil tanker.
There's light between the cars.   ✍

DOING DRUGS IN PARADISE

In the end, they hung him.

It proved a point and you should
know this when entering the country.
A lucky few have someone
waiting for them on the outside.
A lucky few lose only
the unwanted parts of their minds.

The country you are entering
does not tolerate the wholesale sales
of the soul, does not
traffic its children on primetime TV,
will let you go as far as you want to go

in a six by eight cell.
You think your origin of birth
will save you. You haven't thought
very much up till now.

The last person in this cell
scratched their days into Malaysian brick.
The one before that followed a blue dot
into the tunnel, over the hill.
You think all this should make a difference.

Back on the page (a newspaper or whatever)
a zealot gets their story, a publisher
their dime. For seven seconds
democracy looks east
to the rod and the rope, wonders
how the world could be so cruel, takes

another call, places orders,
scratches another day into its droid.

Santa Muerta, Give Me an Open Casket

They do as they will
  in the new Old Mexico, make saints
    that rumble and rattle

in the vein, take heads
  that bounce down pyramids,
    heads that roll

from fast turning cars.
  What was done dark
    in the back of the church

is done dirty on daylight streets.
  Stained glass, tinted glass,
    a theatre of rival and staged death.

Family Business, we'll just call it.
  Life is short like a bullet, so give me
    soldiers, give me boys,

give me girls, a gun between my legs.
  Give me a good looking corpse
    and a two story mausoleum.

You toss gold and roses on my box;

I wail for you and your widows.
　　All is pageant and pesos

and traffic always traffic.
　　The poor must whore, walk
　　　　their trembling children to school.

But don't look to the mothers
　　and the fathers in Washington.
　　　　They *are* the business.　　✍

LEVELING

"I hear America singing in the Yellow Pages."
—Lawrence Ferlinghetti

This is the summer of leveling,
perhaps the sixth extinction, perhaps
the ninth, but who stays to count.
This is the morning it all went up
as usual: the upstage light sending
shadows of the unsuspecting city
down the sloping desert,
over the weed-grown gas stations and
six-sided conference rooms of the Navajo.
This is a library in flames.

Busy at terminals that tick off zeros
and ones like spent species,
the gray aliens of commerce
looked the other way.
Only a few of the warm-bloods
felt the tremors, the inevitable undoing.
They were not conspiracists.
They were lonely as a crowd.
This is creative non-fiction.

Oh, my hundred thousand years,

my walk across the continents, my civilization—
if love is something I can say
I've followed your story
late into the candle-lit night, coffee stains
on the page, chuckles under my breath,
tears, anguish, boredom.

I've nailed the wall time and again
with your hopelessly hysterical volume.
This is me, witnessing.
This is the summer of leveling.
This, perhaps, is the one we survive.   ↜

Turn It The Fuck Off

Run with that TV in your arms. Run
down the street, duck into oblivion.
Run with all the name brands:
the Nike, the Sony, the Apple, the Obama.
Covet the instruments of your slavery.

Run with a 9mm, a blog, a satellite,
an army, the New Church of Your Lord.
Run back to the auction block to sweat
and swagger in your cell.
The steel mills and honest farms
have been replaced with prisons.

Run to The Right, they already
have your name. Run to The Left
where they eat their own children.
Blow up the world
with your magical three piece Jesus.

Into the burning night you run
like crazy with your head cut off—
that's just what they're expecting.
Run with that television
like it's the last bullet to enter your brain. ❧

FROM A CABIN ALREADY GONE
for Mary Elizabeth Van Pelt

Take a last look at wooden spoons on the hill,
wind and smoke through dark logs,
feathers hanging from the beam.
A last look at 1,600 love letters hugging
in cardboard boxes. Say goodbye to cold
grounds at the bottom. Goodbye
to east Tennessee fog lying low so far from home.

This is the West where the snow
must thunder to stick. This was the beginning
of my end, the place where I became
again and again. This here ain't no 2nd rate movie.
I made every walk to the river count.
Goodbye, fox and upturned ducks.

I'm here, not because I'm not there,
but because I came to this high valley
poured and settled like yellow meal
between the peaks. I came
after having gone mad (several times).

The sick we healed did not stand up
and walk. They did not reconcile
on the courthouse steps or in that last rented room.

They cannot find their thanks.
The soup kitchen will be closed.

Yesterday a church on the border
was saved by Bingo. Today my redemption
wants nothing, has gambled everything, plays
all day in the fields behind the house,
comes home when I whistle.
I have other friends here as well.

This is the winter of fresh pencils,
the last walk to Chimayo, the last time
we drag our timbers to the fire.
This is probably not true.
Goodbye, anyway—just in case
they cancel Tennessee,
in case you feel like writing.
My address has never changed.   ❧

DRY DOCK

Rocket ship bumblebee,
spinning asteroid flyby,
    heaving volcanic cleavage.
Today is the new Southwest.

Brunette green of Mesquite;
blonde green of Russian Olive;
redheaded green of Salt Cedar.
Nonnative is a tick in time, yesterday maybe
or some new goodbye.
The mistake is trying to place a city
between ourselves and our calling.

A school of soft-bellied clouds
slips through, passes over remaining cowboys,
meets on the ridge, disperses in silence—
the kind of silence a river knows.

The importance and arogance of others
can't hurt me, but my own
can get in the way.
When I remember I'm a cloud,
    the sky is no big deal.
When I forget, we can have
this conversation anywhere.

My friend, Noor, checks in
to the Desert Motel, grows beard,
tricks wind, lays purple track
toward the Space Port.
    He's got tickets overhead.
I can't see him, but I always wave.

Ocotillo, Cactus Wrens, petrified miners.
Some say these bone-suckin' cities
were never meant to be.
The emulator throws out random code—
some sticks, some doesn't.
Objects in play change, but gravity
likes to hang around.

Wind-washed sand sparkles back
to its maker. Take a last look,
    one reptile to another.
The sea has not forgotten
and may come for us again.
But the desert, the desert
is the incubator of the mind.   ❧

Trees Weep for One Another

> Nine years after the super nova of 1054 a volcano west
> of Chaco filled our world with smoke and rumble and
> refugees. We have seen this before.

Trees are weeping today. The trees are green
and sad. They drink water for those who can't.
They pass on everything they know.
They let the wind have what belongs to the wind.

The trees cry for their families in Arizona
who are being consumed by wildfire.

The news comes to us, the deer come to us,
mountain bluebirds, red tails with ash-dusted wings.
We've seen them before—immigrants on the run.

They stagger across the line, bewildered,
dazed with smoke, without work, without homes.
There is no question about sharing the water.   ⌁

Every Joe and Mary

I'm like most every Joe or Mary.
I play the lottery. I have plans.
Thirty here, Thirty there.

And I know the weight of paper and
I've seen the tops of clouds.
Is it sacrilege to be well traveled?

I arrive at the foot of the hill
and introduce myself. I know the walk;
I know the drill. Get out the blood,
the court order, the goodbyes.
Oh, and yes, the stones.

I've signed up for redemption, mine
and a few friends' that couldn't make it.
I'm a stand-in. I'm a comic.

Evidently I'm not serious enough
about my career. Evidently.
I keep being sent to the back of the line.

Last week I applied for carpenter—
working on the sets.
Now I enter through the back:

coffee breaks, flirting, union dues.
Nobody's buying it.
"We want the old Joe back."

Ah Christ, hold this ticket 'til I return.   ॐ

Leaning Left, Leaning Right, Room for Everything

> "entheogens... make you a person who tries to find balance."
> —Art Goodtimes

I reached into the bag,
pulled up a handful
of dirt-flecked shrooms,
chewed the natural world into filaments
of connecting crystal threads,

inhaled the smoking leaves
and understood every spoken word
of those sunset birds
    coming to roost
in the mountains of Tepoztlan.
I am no stranger to myself.

Leary was wrong; Leary was right.
Chemistry is scaffolding, hyperlinks.
We took the sunshine
and met on the corner,
    spun and giggled
around a stop sign, knowing
it was the drain plug
of the made up world.
The rebel priest said

when Jesus joined the urge within the bang
all matter was infused
       with the possibility
of our waking. All,
then, is sacrament.

So I grabbed an apple from the dash
of my truck, gave myself communion.

The urge outdoes itself,
becomes the next something else,
reaches a hand behind,
       lovingly pulls
the rest of us up—
balance an acre of clouds returning.

The mountain is full
of blooming secrets;
its rivers flow from the sun.
I am a river of enthusiasm. I am
en theos, always in love.   ✍

In the Wave of The Big Dot

I went out connecting
dots dots
that grew from the ruptured crust
the wrinkled teaming face
pinnacles of planet rising
above water into blue later
trembling with bravery
I crawled out at night
more dots

their names I strung
across the void pinning
them to upright rocks I placed
in hollow places
where I stepped back
pointing to myself
newly appointed
I put meaning
on the animals too

I gambled everything
bet my wives my freedom
committed suicide at the end
of every spree
bewildered I retreated

made an altar to retreat
emptiness
the new politic
doing not doing dots
I imagined managing

Coming to life I
gold-leafed goddess and god
where I dreamed them
in their sleep learned
to bathe to figure to chisel
stone into math and glory
investigation held
the light while surgery revealed
that everything comes apart
anything can burn

Bringing light inside
crushing it on stone secretly
longing for sleep I obliterated
reflections offspring ghosts
deemed to be other
obligation guilt blame regret
how's that for games
better than stickball we thought

Beauty had an age behold
all to itself undone we

hollowed out interiors
in awe awe
struck that we had stood
and stood so tall
before beginning to burn
out of air control

So sure that we
singularly
brought down the house crouching
in the sledge of storyteller rant
flood dinosaurs fire distant shores hell
I almost gave up
kill me I tried
but undefined urge
threw me crest of the wave
leaning into next now
my choices perhaps pre-adapt

What's the gossip
all or nothing or
more mumbling
greenhouse incubator waiting
for ticket out of here and
better fuel if love is
the rule rule
from the front of the house
it just feels better

I'm not nearly naked
but less addicted
to the next thing I think turning
in time I see someone past
looking like me here I say
these fading dots belonged
to your family nothing now
but bang bang dust　～

WE BEGIN
from a gathering on the western slope

In the heaving
a small fire
spiral, curl
that curve
known nothing
egg fin
devotee flame

In the heaving
spine thrill
urn flow
enjoin
so much water now
stations to come
ecstatic dome

In the heaving
coming round
recognize
counsel of thirty nine
dream world
nova now
hanging home

In the heaving
evening flutter
all contain
dissolve, decay
think again
joy skin

In the heaving
laser frame
tumbling
grinning green
child's flute
peering rim

In the heaving
spectral spin
travel nod
roadway friends
de-li-cious-ness
again
in the heaving we begin   ❧

THE BLUE CURL WITHIN YOU

THE DISAPPEARANCE OF SANDIA MOUNTAIN

She did not arrive on horseback
nor on the heels
of burning sage ceremonies
but was found standing
in morning's kitchen—the mountain
delphinium blue, clear as a wing.

Yesterday's winds whipped up
the dust of western deserts,
juniper pollen, newly plowed fields,
    and hid the mountain
in a yellow storm—
some secret work going on
behind the veil.

You say she turns away, slips
from your horizon. You say,
    Forsaken. You say, Hazy.
But there, at the window
she stirs, preparing summer.   ✒

Precious Metal to Water

Chemistry is something
to get excited about,
or the other way around.

The code and the carriage
come with their own driver.
    Paint this cave;
live your coordinates.
Rapidly the rain approaches.

You speak of alchemy,
of ghosts in the skin.

This is no singular game
of play pretend—I'm caught
in everybody's body.

The tumblers fall, and all
the chickadees and goshawks
    rise at once.

On the other side of the divide
you chew slowly. Rice,
boll weevils, Aquarian verbs,
directions to the loam.

I've taken your mouth
slowly—one petal at a time.

I've thought up a storm.   ❧

And I've Come to Treasure the Falling

Snow drifting through itself,
twisting
on a wave, sudden fountain
up and over the balcony.
What I don't know.

In another now, I tell myself,
I'm figuring all this out.
I have data and history—
oh, so much.

When I like the sound of *leaning*
everything seems to.
When I see knives
I see them all the way
down the hall.

But snow I hold lightly,
otherwise my ideas
burn the world to a crisp. &

WINTER'S SUCCESSOR

In another room someone shivers
or wrestles or sits up straight
with a knot of covers.
They have proof and plans,
have audited the lives of orphans.
They believe that room.

In a hidey hole under the bushes
army men and tea cups
also believe, believe secretly
no one will come for them.
They toss around words
like crazy, like love, like hate,
like can't and can so.

Outside the word is winter.
What it believes
is the whole day turning
toward enough light
to bring everyone home.   ∽

Press Release

Skip conception
and the hard green part,
go directly to falling pods.
It's not, after all, a lollipop tree
but a sycamore carrying on.

On the charcoal lot below
white stripes tell tenants
where to stall their cars.
Seed pods playing
their own game find spots
outside the lines.

Tires ten thousand times
their size smash the orbs
into fuzzy mass.
Fifty feet above the cars the tree
throws down a few more
for immediate release. ✍

GOING AROUND

You turn in mist, switchback
across the canyon, rise
through still aspen
rutted and rubbed—
a forest of eyes unblinking
through thin white skin.

Nothing looks dirty anymore.
All is smudged.

Wavering on freezing
a morning thaw
has scattered a tumble
of rocks onto the road.

You pause, pleased
to come upon
such honest undoing.   ❧

How the Land Receives Us

Finches, sparrows and doves
chitter-chatter and coo-hoo
blink-eyed into growing pink.

Pale morning ghost of Sandia Peak
runs naked behind Willow and Ash.
Ranges wake along the corridor,

raise their subterranean wings.
Above us: the wide western blue.
Above that: the wheel of the cosmos

turning with births—
experiments similar to our own.
So much throbbing!

A friend calls
with an invitation to her table.
We eat with our hands.

Humus, lamb, olives.
We bring our worlds together:
science, grandbabies, war.

We tell stories of how we arrived;
speak of settlements, strength
in voices, our covenant with water. ❧

Sun Storm
when the compass jumps

And so it seems America,
your are terrified
of darkness and silence—
the very place we wait for you.

You've pushed my family
across the land, chased us
into small poor places with
surround sound, petawatt lamps.

Windblown and weary
we go undetected
in simple ideas, honest desires, yet,
you come for our children.

The map of your coverage
grows by the hour, the blood
from your rapacious shove turns
even the oceans red.

But your laser lights
and walls of chatter cannot dispel
the boogie man. Your distractions
just so much mumbling.

The sun will storm, scatter
your mechanics in a green wind,
quiet the fearful light of false dawn.
We will hear, and we will see again.

And so it seems America,
darkness and silence
were never your enemy,
but the womb of your redemption.   ✑

SPACE KINDLY

> "And to the ship that has led the way time and time
> again we say, 'Farewell, Discovery.'"
> —Josh Byerly/STS-133 Descent Commentator,
> Kennedy Space Center, March 9, 2011

Thrusters and boosters
at any stage roar
with reason for our leaving—
this urge to know, this urge
our passion and our passage.
Darkness, then, a sea
folded upon itself, expanding,
alive when encountered,
empty until seen.

I shuttle
nectar and astronauts
to your floating flower,
bring back
sacred dust, distance,
light in other forms.

Suns rise and suns set—
some nights much shorter than others.

I am your love
going forward. I am
the edge of your darkness.
All is rendezvous in space.   ᕰ

NOTHING BRIDGE

Purple tercets of Wandering Jew
do as cuttings do,
while thin white threads root
in the jelly glass. It is itself.

Found in a dumpster; passed on
by friend; scraped from the board—
take hold where you are.
Step out on nothing,
    on light, on urge.

These are your tendrils.
This is your tongue,
your breath heaving with moon.

I follow morning into dusk,
listen to my dreams.
I wander purple. I am my own flag.

Cut me into billions, cast me
to earth. Show me the cavern,
the missing floor, the caravan.

In the presence of other elders
    I step out on nothing.   ✍

NIGHT ON FIRE

Cool sleep rolls off the shelf.
    Sunlight soaks back into the ground—
        pink, purple, a kind of black.

Flower fragrances pungent-sweet
    call down unmarked trails, dream pockets,
        second worlds. Soon, the moon.

Watch your head—
    this is where it will unravel.
        Fireflies on the desert

are stars bleeding through the veil.
    Their business may already be done.
        Every time I blink they disappear,

return, our clocks set
    by the same empty hand.
        In another night with friends

I flash hello across a meadow,
    constellations adrift. We recognize
        one another by our shine. ∽

In the Trees

The dappled sun tosses here.
I've never seen this, exactly,
such eagerness to be a morning—
a shoot of leaves, tomorrow a rambling branch.
I've cut and stacked these friends.

Over the hill someone saws his way toward me.
When we finally meet
there'll be nothing left to burn.
We're already home, this wind or the next.

What she knows from the Bible
is that children are slain upon a stone.
What trembles in her hand is the knife
with which she cuts the cord.
Is this your new lover calling
above the burning street?
Is this the last drop of ice?

We pretend a straight line with sides
but even the eyes must die.
Then it's me whirling with my arms out,
then it's you.
The light plays on our faces,
a caterpillar chews all the way to the edge.   ✺

See Beauty Done

In this lucky life I ask:
    how can I walk in beauty.
        I see the tree as the sky between leaves.

I raise my arms and run next to the sun.
    Look at me, my child voice sings, look at me;
        I'm legs and hands and breath and dirt.

I'm hot in the center, a rainbow fusion.
    I'm water on the wind.
        Say but the word and see it done.

Miracles cavort in silence;
    it's the void that carries the count.
        All the trees are inside, all

the chewed grass, the yearning fish,
    the way beneath the mountain.
        What, then, could darkness be? ✑

RED YES

A yawn of rose-orange light
splashes the wall, the floor, flows
over stacks of half eaten books
and the night dreams that evaporate
like frescoes in a newly opened cave.

A red morning calls to cities that rise
perpendicular to the sea that spawned them, calls
to island civilizations that tie nets and drive taxis
with volcanic precision, to ships returning
from deep space, and to the traveller
crossing the dirt road in front of her house.
This red morning.

You are the morning of the newest sun,
the lover within the lover, the one
I am always facing.
We are ruined together.
I have been upright for eight minutes;
I have been upright for three million years.
I am barely a moment away.
I, also, am red.

This morning I will meet someone new
and ask them with small hinting words

if they too are as large as they seem,
if they too are red and overflowing.
And even if they try to lie,
their eyes will say, yes.

WAVES IN THE WING

Now and then a bird flies through.
It perches here, silently.
It caws
like a train making time.
It's black, then red.

It's white and soft where the moon begins.
It has no regrets about
its relationship with the wind.
Now and then you throw back a sash.
A bird peering.

There are waves in the wing.
The one you keep making.
Wave making you.
There's a bird I can't see,
a warrior on the coast, an old rattler
living out what's left.

It's the redemption of the visits.
Otherwise
it's another network or war.
Beauty like the curve of a scimitar.
Now and then a bird flies through.

Stepping In

I live beside a great river.
I live with this enormous sky overhead.
I walk among the trees.
Am I known here?

I am yearning and turmoil. I am
something happening next
in all this wonder.
I want to hide from the wind.

I want to pull the wind apart
and step into myself.

I live to go down
singing in the space between,
in the wetness of your water, the timber
and urge of your voice.

I sing and sign and cry with your mouth.
I want what the wind wants.   &

Blue Green Jewel

Mouths ready, eyes wide,
we wait for rain.
When the moment comes
everything opens.
And that's the end of it—
the long waiting.

And that's the beginning of it—
the gulping and gulping,
thanking and thanking,
cupped hands and handing
of cups to one another.
And that's the way of it.

This blue green jewel
is our one clear eye.
The water we are
is the love we love. We
rain and gulp and thank
and rain again...

And that's how it is
to live as a jewel.   ✍

Follow Hawk

The sky here moves. We walk
with each other. The rock has opened
on our behalf—this, then, our song.

For all the world we have fallen;
to begin is to fail. We are here
in the same river, in the same time.

I visit you. As your brother
my hands have bled and mountains
curved for my word. *Harm was never.*

Trees and worms live among us, fly
between our dreams. Closer
than you think, they love.

The earth beneath us calls for feet.
The ones who come close touch
and are free to follow the highest hawk. ✑

Because We Are the Wave

We skate on supple skin,
a fragile mindset,
collection of agreements.

Yesterday we ate the apple
and learned how it fell;
at high noon we split it in two

a million times over.
Surely some among us
will wake, will ride

the wave of enlightened flight.
Surely, you feel
the blue curl within you.   ⁓

ABOUT THE AUTHOR

Born and partly raised in eastern Oklahoma, at the age of seventeen Stewart Warren became a convicted felon. He holds no university degrees. Neither of these details have hindered his passions nor his abilities to be a writer and a teacher. Quite the contrary.

Earlier in his life Stewart travelled in Canada, the U.S. and Mexico, catching rides at truck stops, small plane terminals and along farm to market roads while working his way through a variety of cultures and landscapes. In more recent decades he has settled into small migrations through southern Colorado and northern New Mexico, following an "unseen friend" on a path of self discovery and camaraderie with fellow travellers.

Stewart is author of eight poetry collections and is published in various journals and anthologies. His poetry is both personal and transpersonal with a mystic undercurrent. As a publishing coach and an organizer of community events, Stewart assists others in deepening their creative experience and realizing their artistic visions.

www.heartlink.com

www.ingramcontent.com/pod-product-compliance
Lightning Source LLC
Chambersburg PA
CBHW051825040426
42447CB00006B/371